SADDLE UP

and R-I-I-I-D-E

More Cowboy Poetry

By JIM ROSS

Enjoy the ride!
Jim Ross

D0066905

Cover and Illustrations by
M.J. ROSS

Additional copies available from the author at:
3030 Homeacres Rd., Stevensville, MT 59870.

Other Poetry Books by JIM ROSS

"Get Down And Come In"
(Out of Print)

"Pull Up A Chair"
(In Second Printing)

PRINTED IN THE UNITED STATES OF AMERICA

ISBN 0-961793228

DEDICATED—

To the girl who hitched double harness
With an unlikely teammate such as me;
Who has pulled her share of the load
And remains as content as can be.

And to our five children,
Corbin, Mary Jane, Joe, Rob and Jan

And to our grandchildren

And to Mary's and my parents (R.O. and Anna
Briggs and Joe and Elsie Ross) who were
responsible for making our union possible. ⌐

ACKNOWLEDGEMENTS

The author would like to give special credit to his daughter, Mary Jane Ross, for her artistic endeavors in this book, as well as in his two previous books. Her drawings depict most accurately the stories he tells, and add immeasurably to them. Without her art work this book would lose a valuable assist.

A special thanks is also given to his wife, Mary, not only for her assist in his writings, but also for her encouragement to "keep it up".

A thanks also goes to the rest of the family and others for their encouragement, and to those many who have written encouraging letters. Son-in-law Donald Burgess deserves a special thanks for his assists.

Finally, the author would like to offer his thanks to Advanced Litho Printers, Great Falls, Montana for their fine work and great cooperation in the printing of his books. ⊔

CONTENTS

CONTENTS—Continued

SADDLE UP AND R-I-I-I-D-E

When you wake up in the morning
  And the birds are all a-twitter,
When the sun is just arising
  With the mountain peaks a-glitter,
When your body feels like playing,
  Why not make the day a getter,
So saddle up and r-i-i-i-d-e.

If your pony nickers at you
  When he hears you roust about,
If he nuzzles at your shoulder
  With a friendly brush of snout,
Sure those oaties that you pour him
  Will transform to body clout,
So saddle up and r-i-i-i-d-e.

When the world is getting to you,
  Life is taking of its toll,
There is no better therapy
  For your body and your soul
Than to visit with your pony
  As he canters round a knoll,
So saddle up and r-i-i-i-d-e.

*It's a tonic that
grows on you.*

PICKY, PICKY, PICKY

A strange rider stopped at mealtime
  To pass the time of day;
He was invited in to luncheon,
  His horse got oats and hay.

As they gathered round the table
  The cook served a tuna dish;
Said the rider to the hostess;
  "That looks to me like fish."

"I'm not akin to fishy stuff,
  It's beef that suits this drover;"
The hostess answered to the point:
  "Then your lunch today is over."

As told to me by friend John Carlson.
Bravo to Mary Kay.

ME AND MY PONY

Just a ridin', ridin', ridin', across the
    western plains,
My spurs are makin' music, it's circulatin'
    through my veins;
The meadowlarks are singin', the coyote
    had his say,
Two hoot-owls have announced the comin' of
    the day;
The bluestem grass is belly deep, there's
    dewdrops on the sage,
These foothills 'long 'bout daylight are
    an orange and purple rage.

Just a joggin', joggin', joggin', my pony's
    lean and stout,
A movin' through this native grass, he knows
    his way about;
On a rope a bustin' steers or in the herd
    cuttin' out,
He will best them heel-to-toe or a goin'
    snout-to-snout;
He savvies well the cow game, you don't
    have to show him twice,
It's Eden to be on him, he's a cowboy's
    paradise.

Just a rockin', rockin', rockin', in my old
 Heiser kack,
It fits just like it growed there, upon my
 pinto pony's back;
'Hind the cantle is a bedtarp, a soogan in
 between,
Plus fryin' pan and coffee pot, some bacon
 and a bean;
A slicker and a carbine, and I'm ridin'
 mighty tall,
It's fifty miles to stompin' grounds, we'll
 be there by nightfall.

Just a dreamin', dreamin', dreamin', a-snooze
 last night 'neath the sky,
The air was crisp as autumn, countless stars
 glowed bright on high;
I dreamed a dream of heaven, what it holds
 that's truly best,
When morning came I recognized, 'twas all
 right here out west;
So when I change my grazin' sound the bugles,
 drum and fife,
There should only be rejoicin', I've had the
 best there is in life.

It is me and my old pony, livin' higher
  every day,
Wouldn't trade a foot of prairie for a world
  of brick and clay;
There is romance in the open, God keeps
  nature all in check,
I'll play the cards He dealt me, don't want
  any from the deck. ↵

*Put this together while on a
trip home from the prairie
country of eastern Montana.*

A STAR IS BORN or
FROM SLEW WATER TO BOURBON

He was just a drifter passin' through,
  I found him all tattered and torn;
I took Sam in and vowed to see
  If a cowpoke couldn't be born.

I gave him a shirt and neckerchief,
  And for ten bucks I bought him boots;
A Stetson we plucked outa the mud
  From in front of the buckin' chutes.

We wrapped his legs in Levi garb
  And bowed 'em a bit at the knee;
Chaps and spurs we found at the pawn,
  Then he whistled a tune of glee.

He looked the part of a buckaroo
  Who had come to town for a spree,
So he staked a claim at the Mint saloon
  For the wise and folly to see.

Soon comes a dude dressed Hollywood style,
  A bag full of greenbacks in tow;
He offers Sam a wad of the stuff
  To be star in a western show.

He writes up a contract with flourishes,
  And advances a chunk of the dough;
Sam will make it to stardom sure
  If a handlebar lip he can grow.

He says he likes this cowpoke game.
  "It sure beats ridin' the rails";
Still his apprehension shows a bit
  When he thinks about forkin' broomtails.

But belly up to the mahogany, boys,
  Sam's buyin' whiskey for the house;
And nobody cares that he knows not
  A horse from a nanny goat's spouse. ⌐

*My wife thought I should
title this poem "A Star Is
Born" but I prefer "From
Slew Water to Bourbon."*

EVEN A COWBOY CAN CRY

If you don't think a cowboy cries
    Just watch the dew form in his eyes
When an old friend gets sick and dies
    And he must say his last goodbyes.

Or when his top horse bites the dust,
    As soon or late all ponies must;
Then's when those dew drops swell and bust,
    Flow down those saddened cheeks of crust.

When that bull calf from his prize cow
    Gets weak and wastes away somehow,
That lump within gets hard and now
    True sadness shows upon his brow.

Or when that late spring blizzard blows,
    Snuffs out most of his cattle throws.
Piled in ravines or 'gainst fence rows,
    And just plain starved to death or froze.

When the price of beef drops through the floor,
    Aft' he has spent his wad and more
On dogie spread he'd worked years for,
    Then banker 'friend' shows him the door.

Then's when he needs a loving wife
    To wipe the tears of recent strife;
To heal the sting of ordeal's knife,
    And reinstill his spark for life.

His tears may not be visible,
    His sobs not heard nor felt, but still
His innards churn like that windmill,
    And his sad heart sure beats to kill.

Cowboys can take a loss or gain,
  Prone to accept sunshine or rain,
However God sings the refrain,
  But still they sure can feel the pain.

*Cowboys are a rugged lot, but
generous and good hearted.
They have feeling for both
man and beast.*

TOO GOOD TO SELL

Somewhere out there on the prairie
  Is a pony I used to know,
Though he wears my J Cross iron
  He's as free as the drifting snow.

We partnered on many a roundup,
  We busted a slew of them steer,
We hazed for bulldogging cowboys
  And garnered our share of the cheer.

But times have to change, as we know,
  And there came of that time for me,
I had not a place to keep him
  So elected to turn him free.

It didn't seem right to sell him
  In spite of the price he would bring,
I despaired to think that another
  Might let him feel some cruelty sting.

So I took him down in the breaks
  Where once he was known to dwell,
And there in a vast wild area
  I bade him my fondest farewell.

I slipped the hackamore from him,
  He snorted and bolted the air,
He raced the ridge in the sunset,
  Then turned and gave me a stare;

Just as if to say, "Old Partner,
  I'll see you in the Sweet Beyond,
I've enjoyed each minute with you
  And I'll treasure our mutual bond."

Now several years have expired
  Since he was last seen by this friend,
I've heard he's among the wild ones
  A-grazing that big river bend.

I know if he heard my whistle,
  Be it today, next spring or fall,
He'd come and nuzzle my shoulder,
  Then follow me into the stall.

I'd give him a bucket of oaties
  And a forkful of fresh wild hay,
With friendship restored between us
  As it was in our yesterday.

Then if our callings from the Lord
  Should come in the same pouch of mail,
I'd saddle him and we'd check stock
  As we travel that distant trail.

Nostalgia often overtakes a fella when he starts thinking about those saddle ponies in his life.

THE EXTREMES

You have heard the old saying
  about feast or famine;
And the fisherman says,
  "It is sucker or salmon."
But when you're out on the range
  drinkin' all kinds of juice,
If it's not constipation
  you are bound to be loose. ↵

Alkali water has put many a cowboy to looking for a tall sagebrush.

LIL AND THE RED DAWG SALOON

Howlers were in tune at the Red Dawg Saloon
  On the banks of the Bitterroot,
The boardwalk outside was alive and astride
  With many a high heeled boot.

Blackjack and stud poker was played with a joker,
  And the sevens and snake-eyes did roll,
For the cowboys and miners, loggers and diners
  'Twas their favorite watering hole.

Now a filly named Lil in her lace and her frill
  Was a regular greeter of sorts,
Her eyes were abore on that batwing door
  In search of the well heeled sports.

When she heard a spur jingle she felt a nerve tingle
  In her bosom so well endowed,
She'd greet him in style with her enchanting smile,
  Then usher him in through the crowd.

Now Lil was a dame with a gorgeous frame
  And a cavernous cleavage, you bet,
A garter rode high, well up on her thigh,
  And her jewelry with diamonds was set.

But if you thought her a floozy, an immoral Susie,
  She would kiss you a quick bye-and-bye,
She was sweet little Lil with her eye on the till,
  Just promotin' the scotch and the rye.

Once Lil got too bold in her searchin' for gold
  As she hurried her man to the bar,
She received a black eye from the wife of the guy
  And forever she wore the scar.

Now once Lil was wed to a herder named Ted,
  Top dog in a sheepherding crew,
She worked the drop band and made a good hand,
  But soon tired of mutton stew.

A cowboy came along just singin' a song,
  A yodelin' the whole day through;
She packed her war bag and boarded his nag,
  Then they rode off into the blue.

Their life was a ball and he gave it his all
  'Till a horse named Shipwreck did him in,
She was holdin' his head when he softly said:
  "I am goin' to pay for my sin."

Then along came a miner who treated her finer
  Than the gold dust in his poke,
When his claim petered out he went driftin' about
  With some other prospectin' folk.

Lil soon found her niche, it was servin' a ditch
  At the bar in the Red Dawg Saloon,
She made lots of dough and it didn't come slow,
  She could lure in the rich and the loon.

'Twas a Saturday night the crowd got so tight
  It drank that old bar plumb dry,
That saloon got so hot it burned down on the spot
  And even brave Lil had to cry.

Thus ended the boon of the Red Dawg Saloon,
  But its legend will long live on,
Next morn at daylight there appeared on the site
  A sign simply reading "Dawg gone." ↵

The Red Dawg saloon and the
sign "Dawg Gone" are true;
the rest may or may not be
true.

DEAR LORD

I'd be glad to 'cash in' in my wagon,
    'Tween the soogans snug in my bed,
Using my slicker for pillow,
    With my bed tarp pulled near my head.

I'd like my last meal to be beans,
    With a little sow belly thrown in;
A biscuit with jam of gooseberry,
    And java in my coffee tin.

Camped near the Musselshell River,
    In the shade of those old Bull Hills;
Where the sun and rains spill heaven
    And paint the draws with daffodils.

Where the meadows are rich with bluestem,
    And the hills have that sweet pine scent;
Where the springs run fresh cool water,
    And there's quiet and deep content.

There is where I spent my youthhood,
    There is where I'd like to lie down;
Far off from the life of glitter,
    Far away from the lights of town.

So if you have no objections,
    I'll return to that fertile land;
There you can check and assess me
    For your own or Lucifer's brand.

*The Musselshell was a very
popular grass country in the
days of the early stockman.*

AIM TO PLEASE

When your reputation's questioned
  And you must defend the same,
Always shoot 'em in the right eye,
That will sure disturb their aim. ↵

KEEP THE FAITH

Though it be cloudy out today,
  The sun is shining anyway;
It may be hidden from your view
  But still it's shining just like new.
This should be solace for us all
  On gloomy day of strife and pall;
If God can keep the sun a-shine
  He can cure the woes of yours and mine. ↵

Blackbird on an old cow's rump
  Waiting for a louse to jump. ↵

One old magpie sittin' on a fence
  Tryin' to make a dollar out of fifteen cents. ↵

Some old, some new,
All put to rhyme
Just for you.

A RELIC OF THE PAST

Behind the corral in sort of a heap
  Is a home like I used when I once herded sheep;
The roof is all gone, the sides in decay,
  The floor and the wheels are just rotting away.

The old doubletrees the horses hitched to
  Have long gone the way that good antiques do;
The tongue is a wreck, been all shortened up,
  Appears to have been stubbed for a modern pickup.

The bunk in the back where the herder slept
  And the bin underneath where the spuds were kept
Are weathered in place, like the table leg,
  And the outside shelf for the water keg.

The shelf over the bunk is still intact,
   But the glass in the window is loosened and cracked;
The hinged down door to the cupboard there
   Served as a table, a bench was the chair.

In the near corner next to the old door
   Is that sheepherder stove all rusted with lore;
Baked the best biscuits, cooked the tastiest stew,
   Boiled better coffee than Mother could brew.

The overhead bows are good to this day,
   But the canvas cover has wasted away;
The lantern for light is still hanging there,
   With a candle nearby as a needed spare.

Hasp on the door is latched with a stick,
   Strangers could enter with nary a trick,
Could stir up a meal to their own desire:
   "Just clean up their mess, leave wood for a fire."

The last herder's camp I saw out on the range
   Was shiny, it glistened, it looked mighty strange;
With gas and refrig, who could dream of the like,
   And beside it was parked a Suzuki bike. ↳

*When I herded sheep from a
wagon back in the early '30s
I felt lucky to have a horse
for transportation.*

DEAR DOCTOR

I sure hate bothering a man like you,
   But this cowboy is in an awful stew;
I've not penned a note since my daddy died,
   Still my feelings are such that I can't hide.

Since taking Elixer, it's done wonders for me,
   There's a glint in my eye, a spring in my knee;
I'm ninety years old and terrible in love,
   I so want to marry my turtle-dove.

She's just twenty-five, a chick of delight,
   But I must confess a degree of fright;
My good friends advise that such an engage
   Just might prove fatal, this diff'rence in age.

Our affair is torrid, what shall I do?
   I'll wait with intent an answer from you.
Please hurry it up, and I will abide,
But we so want to wed, I want a bride.

It wasn't too long there came in the mail
   An envelope posted from Doc MacPhail;
Slim scanned the letter, then read it aloud
   To his concerned friends, that revered crowd.

"Take the Elixer and double the dose,
   Marry the maiden, then hold her real close;
Treat her as equal and query no whys,
   Let nature prevail, if she dies, she dies." ↵

Just a little innocent humor.
Haven't heard that she died
yet.

THE GREAT ONES

What's in a horse's name you ask,
   And just how did they come to be?
Well, my Keno, Babe and Daisy
   Were a prize trio, team of three;
They sure could turn the virgin sod
   Pulling against that triple-tree.

They would lean into the collar,
   Thick leather traces ever tight;
Never quitting of the furrow,
   They puffed and slaved with all their might;
Labored in those hames and harness
   From start of day 'till near the night.

These old buddies of my bygone days
   Helped teach me the farming game;
Bright heavy oats three times a day
   And they would answer to their name;
They earned their place, if there be one,
   In the harness horse hall of fame.

Likewise I've had some saddle stock
   That love for them time cannot dim;
Show stock beside my cow pony
   Would wither in the dust of him;
Some mounts are way above the rest,
   Tough and smart in both mind and limb.

Dusty, Whistler, Red and Freddie
  Were each one cut from special dies;
When I think of these four ponies
  It brings a mist unto my eyes;
May they all be in the cavvies
  Of good horsemen in the skies.

*A well treated horse is right
up there with dogs as 'man's
best friend'.*

THE WAY IT USED TO BE

As I spill juice on a scratch pad
    Recording my thoughts of the day,
I dream of the times that have been
    And cowboying the olden way.

When transportation was a horse,
    And ranches were the open range;
When chow was beans and sow-belly,
    And a good bed felt mighty strange.

When a saddle served dual purpose,
    'Twas ever its owner's delight;
All day it shielded his backside
    And cradled his head at night.

When a rope was made of rawhide,
    Used for catching and as a whip;
When saddles were mostly slick forks
    With scant little for knees to grip.

When a man could start at Fort Worth,
    And ride clear to the Musselshell,
With nary a fence to gaze on,
    No noise machine to break the spell.

Just herding cattle from Texas,
    Up the Bozeman or Chisholm trail;
Fighting blizzard, lightning and rainstorm,
    And quicksand and dust without fail.

Up at the dawn to ride all day,
    And then taking one's turn at night;
Crooning lullabies to those bedded,
    Just a trying to soothe their fright.

The Big Dipper timed the night shifts
  As it rotated round the North Star;
And Cookie called, "Come and get 'er,"
  While the daylight was yet afar.

Rank broncs were eared down for mounting,
  Then the rider'd say, "Let 'er buck;"
If he valued his where-with-all
  He had better not come unstuck.

If a horse broke-in-two on circle
  And the rider got dumped on the damp,
He tried to hang on to the reins
  Cause 'twas a long walk back to camp.

They slept among the rattlesnakes,
  Breathed the scent of sweet prairie sage;
They traveled by sun in the daylight,
  And at night the stars were their gauge.

Guns were not packed for aggression,
  But defense and killing a 'crip';
A slicker and wooly chaps were
  A wardrobe on each winter's trip.

Most cowboys today are rodeo stock
  Asked to ride eight seconds on sight;
They eat three squares, have fancy gear,
  And sleep in the warmth every night.

I'm not funning today's cowboys,
  Just comparing them to the past,
When a hoss, topped off at daylight,
  Was then rode all day if he'd last.

There also were times of pleasure
  In doing the work in life's plight,
Helling it up in Dodge City,
  Singing 'round the campfire at night.

Those cowboys were tough as bull brier,
  And there is no denying it's true;
But when one was down on his luck
  His friends would always come through.

The same goes of modern cowpokes,
  That's a creed they all understand;
It serves the cowboy profession
  Like none other in our fair land. ↵

*Times change but not always
for the best.*

THAT BLUEBERRY ROAN

Horses are a lot like humans,
    They share distinctive traits;
But Flanigan, as I recall,
    Was the worst of reprobates.

My memory might deceive me,
    But good points I cannot glean;
He ne'er displayed a decent streak,
    Neither was he really mean.

He was hard to catch and bridle,
    He always fought the bit;
If a lariat got near his tail
    He'd throw an awful fit.

That flea-bit hide of his was loose,
    He'd slip the blanket sure;
He'd swell up tight against the cinch,
    We never found a cure.

He seldom bucked or ran away,
    But kept a wary gaze;
He'd shy at any sound or sight,
    He liked to move sideways.

He was snaky, spooky, skittish,
    He couldn't quite stand still;
If you rode him relaxed and free
    You might just take a spill.

At rattler's buzz or cricket chirp
    He'd sure stir up a fuss;
He'd jump at grouse or cottontail,
    Just an aggravatin' cuss.

Once Dad was riding home from town
    With sack of flour across the horn;
As he emerged from 'tween the trees
    He cussed the day that horse was born.

The moon was bright and yellow,
    Flan' spied his shadow to his back;
He jumped at least a good twelve feet
    And spilled that flour sack.

Now times were tough and flour was dear,
    Therein that horse had sealed his fate;
Dad vowed to use him just once more
    It would be for coyotee bait.

But we were short a harness horse
    So Dad tried him in the traces;
He earned his oats and saved his hide
    But he ne'er regained our graces. ↵

*He would fight the bit until
he got his tongue over it,
and then go half crazy until
rebridled.*

ON A WHIM

Modern bunkhouses nowadays
  Have jalopies parked far and near;
They don't only dim the landscape,
  They clutter up the atmosphere.

We rail against those iron steeds,
  The stench and noise those clunkers spew!
And dream of when it wasn't so,
  When a good horse would see you through.

Horses live on grass and water,
  What passes through goes in the soil;
It nurtures future spears of grass,
  Leaves no environmental spoil.

You do not feed a horse with hose,
  Nor grease their wheels or steering kit;
To start them you don't pull a choke,
  Then listen to them cough and spit.

Their retreads don't need siping,
  Sparking plugs aren't in their hide;
But they have spark and vim aplenty,
  And surely they have power-glide.

Their tailpipes don't go rusting out,
  Nor do they harm that ozone screed;
They paw for feed when snow is deep,
  And anti-freeze they sure don't need.

I'm not switching from my ponies
  Cause I prefer to go first class;
I'll fork a saddle 'till I die
  Astride a critter that eats grass.

But please harken of my story,
  I have diversified today;
Spent my hard earned summer's wages,
  Bought a Twenty-nine Model-A. ↵

*It's pure and simple
nostalgia, and I love
it.*

TO JOHN L.

Saddles, boots and horses,
  A cowboy tall and lean;
Riding o'er the skyline
  On ranch that's yet pristine.

You loved this high country,
  Your home along the way;
You left it temporarily,
  But now you're home to stay.

Cattle was your choosing,
  You learned the critters well;
Weight and price appraisals
  Is where you did excel.

No favors did you ask,
  A chance was all you sought;
You ground it out and earned
  All that your life has wrought.

First love was your family,
  But ne'er forgot a friend;
And were 'cumulating them
  Right to the very end.

Well you served your country,
  With valor signed and sealed;
Few others earned commissions
  While on the battlefield.

We salute you, John, old pard,
  We keenly feel the loss;
Now riding for our Maker,
  With saddle, boots and hoss.

As you pick your cavvy
  Choose an extra mount or two,
'Cause with some luck we might
  Just end up there with you.

And if we do, my friend,
  A bit of time we'll share
Comparing notes on journeys
  To God's lush range up there.

Until that time arrives
  We'll tend to things down here;
Family, friends and home ranch,
  The things you held most dear. ↵

*First met John at White Sulphur
Springs in 1946. A real good
hand and a fine friend.*

MY OLD WHITEY

They say a white horse is tender,
   Can't stand a full circle ride;
"Partner, I'll tell you they're crazy,
   'Cuz mine can take it in stride."

They say a white horse lacks ribcage,
   Their lungs are inferior when born;
But my old Whitey is rugged,
   And as fresh at night as at morn.

They say a white horse is short lived,
   By the time he's smooth mouth'd he's done;
My old Whitey is thirty-five
   And still good from sun to sun.

White horses are prone to injury,
   I heard say in a roundup spiel;
But my Whitey ain't never had ringbone,
   Or spavin, stringhalt or grease heel.

No glanders or farcy or strangles,
   And heaves he's just never met;
He sure ain't ever had them bots,
   And he's never been near a vet.

I'm never bothered with 'cut-backs'
   When Whitey helps me with stock;
They move along like ants to honey,
   It's true pleasure for this old jock.

This morning I needed to cowboy,
   It was time to move the steers;
So I grabbed old Whitey, that white granite pail,
   With pellets that sing in their ears. ⌐

*When you're short on saddle
ponies, as I am these days,
it is a good way to move
stock.*

ANGORA WOOLY CHAPS

Oh, you relics of the past,
  Nobody wears you anymore;
But your place in western archives
  Is richly laced with cowboy lore.

You were practical and comely,
  Served with distinction and a flair;
You were tuxedos in the bunkhouse,
  You old chaps with wooly hair.

A cowboy dressed in woolies
  Just somehow stole the show,
In the moonlight or the sunshine
  He took on a radiant glow.

No, nothing drew attention
  To a cowboy mounted there,
Riding cirlce or parading,
  As much as chaps with wooly hair.

You weren't just pomp and glitter,
  Though your looks might so portray;
You were worn in self-defense
  Against the hazards of the day.

When in a blinding snowstorm,
  Or 'mong the din of thunderclaps,
You were assuring with your warmth,
  You old angora wooly chaps.

You have wallowed in corral dung,
  Smelled the singe of hair and hide;
You have clung to saddle leather
  On many an outlaw ride.

You have heard the tales of cowboys,
  Some were tall and rank and rare;
Too bad you can't repeat them,
  You old chaps with wooly hair.

Regardless of your color,
  Red or brown or black or white,
You and owner struck a kinship,
  You were essential day or night.

Cowpunching lost some romance
  When barb wire fenced the gaps,
And cowboys lost some lustre
  When they quit wearing wooly chaps.

Until all those oldtime cowboys
  Take their final starlit naps,
You'll be remembered with affection
  As just plain old wooly chaps.

When that roll is called in heaven
  There will be cowboys there, perhaps;
They'll be swapping mounts and saddles
  But seldom ever wooly chaps. ⌐

*Still remember those white
angoras made by Connolly
Bros. in Billings that I
wore as a youngster.*

BEEF OR MUTTON

Guess I am sort of out of date
   In this here cow game nowadays;
I don't savvy all the lingo,
   Nor modern beef producin' ways.

You can buy and sell on futures
   To hedge your profits, so they say;
But my net gains in recent years
   Wouldn't buy a loin fillet.

They've nylon ropes and piggin' strings,
   And fancy medicines galore;
Squeezin' chutes and calf tables,
   And cow and horse docs by the score.

A feeding team is ancient vintage,
   They now feed with dual-drive trucks;
And cavvies all soon shed a horse
   That likes his frolics and his bucks.

But what galls me 'neath my collar
   Is the gear modern cowboys wear;
Speakin' of pride, they've lost it sure,
   I cannot help but blush and stare.

A recent fad they have picked up
   They got from sheepmen, by jinks;
What used to be just lambin' chaps
   Are referred to now as "chinks".

Chinks: A shortened version of cowboy chaps.

*Just felt the need to jab
those modern cowfolk a
little.*

IT'S IRRITATIN'

I'd been feelin' kinda peaked
  Since gettin' bucked off on my head,
Then a rangy steer embarrassed me
  And put me smack in bed.

I had him by the nostrils
  Pourin' linseed oil down his craw,
But when he thought he had enough
  He began to snort and paw.

Soon he tiptoed o'er my innards,
  I got trampled on and sassed;
He was spewin' stuff all over me.
  Oil moves through steers real fast.

When he finally shed my lasso
  He took off on the run;
I raised up on my bruised all-fours
  Hankerin' awful for my gun.

I hobbled to the bunkhouse
  And fell upon a cot;
I was covered with that barnyard stuff,
  My hair was full of snot.

About noon my wife came lookin',
  I ain't showed up for my lunch;
With my breakfast eggs still coolin',
  I guess she felt a hunch.

Well, she looked me over careful,
  Then she called the vet, by damn;
She related I was wheezin' hard
  And looked like spoiled spam.

Doc came lopin' up real pronto,
   He allers does to cure the sick;
He was packin' hose and rumen pump
   Along with a proddin' stick.

Now my thinkin' it was hazy,
   And I'm not hearin' up to snuff;
So my answers to his questions,
   He just took as so much guff.

He checked my lungs and tonsils,
   Then auditioned my old ticker;
It was racin' like a sputnik,
   My breath faintly smelled of likker.

I was sober as a gate post,
   Just nipped the jug to ease the pain;
It dulled my mental hurtin'
   So I nipped and nipped again.

He related somethin' 'bout my stool,
   My milkin' stool, thinks me;
I told him it was pretty loose,
   After all these years it orta be.

Then he queried 'bout my stream,
   Was it at least of pencil size?
He checked both ears and thyroid glands,
   And shot a light beam in my eyes.

He couldn't find a major wrong,
   Said time heals most ever'thing,
And I should feel about like new
   Come green grass in the spring.

So he left me bolus pills,
  Said they're great at curin' footrot;
"Maybe they will cure your gout
  If that is what you've got."

Next time I get humiliated,
  If it's a colt and steer again,
I'll take my lickin' like a man
  And cash my chips right in. ⊔

*Finally learned to be careful
with snuffy colts and salty
steers; it has saved me many
a bruise.*

ONE MORE REQUEST, OH LORD

Guess it's time I started sayin'
  What's been on my mind a while;
Just how grateful I am to You
  For my long life and for its style.

I wouldn't trade these sagebrush fields
  For all the wealth in Knoxville's vault;
Sure the folks who drive Ferraris
  Don't distinguish sweets from salt.

I'd sooner sit a rawhide kack
  Than a mohair bucket seat;
I'd sooner rein my old cowhorse
  Than buzz down an asphalt street.

I'd sooner pack my saddle bags
  Than have those bags beneath my eyes;
I'd sooner live my simple life
  Than be like those Wall Street guys.

So I sure do want to thank You
  For planting my two feet out West;
And for giving me the judgment
  To recognize it as the best.

Where the sky is blue and global,
  And the sun shines bright by day;
Where the waters still run crystal,
  Stars glisten in the Milky Way.

Where there's still a little freedom
  In our movements and our thought;
Where we see Your vast creations
  Without too much that man has wrought.

I'm content with what You've given
  This gray haired cowboy on the wane;
Life has been a total pleasure,
  I want to thank You once again.

There's one more thing I'll ask of You
  While this old Stetson's off my head;
Please steer me to Your great Up Yonder,
  Don't make me shovel coal instead.

                                Amen

Had this poem titled "One Last Request, Oh Lord" but soon found that a bit too confining.

CROONIN' TO THE DOGIES

There's not a bucket yet been found
   That can carry a tune for me;
There's no schoolmarm lit my pathway
   So's I can sing a ding-a-lee.

My music box was born plumb flawed,
   It cannot pitch a tune, no way;
But I can sing to snoozin' steers,
   And on that old bedground they stay.

Steers are said to be color blind,
   But they can hear a croon alright,
And if they do not like the tone
   They'll darn sure soon be out of sight.

Those steers are used to the music
   Of hoot-owls and the coy-o-tee;
So they just think my lull-a-bies
   Are one of them a bit off key.

Singing keeps my spirits climbing,
   And those bovines like the sound;
If I could not have sung to steers
   I'd not kept bunkin' on the ground.

I quit night herding a while back,
   Gave up leading that life so free;
I leased a little dogie spread,
   Took on a wife and family.

But my wife don't like my singin',
   My kids call it abuse, neglect;
So I'm goin' back to trailin' steers
   Where I can get deserved respect.

*Those dogies might like
it better if I could
pack a tune.*

IT CAME TO PASS AT DUFFY'S

I was at Duffy's havin' gin
  When this here stranger saunters in;
As his eyes made their wary probe
  I friendlies up, says, "My name's Job."

I offers him a bit of cheer,
  Some gin or bourbon, scotch or beer;
He said, "Thanks," but allows to how
  He drinks the juice just of a cow.

He said his name was Charlie C.,
  But names don't mean that much to me,
So I gives him a bit of news
  About the path that milk pursues.

"You sip that milk, it tastes right good,
  About like God and motherhood;
It slithers down your gully pipe
  Into your craw where it get ripe.

That milk it soon becomes a cheese,
  Then the fat separates, by jeez;
These glycerides and acids mix,
  And lactose then provides the kicks.

That sugar it goes round and round,
  And in with enzymes it is ground;
With heat applied, and touch of gall,
  It turns to mash and alcohol."

Charlie mulled this over in his mind,
  He scratched his head for clue to find;
He fought the facts as they might be,
  Then with conviction said to me:

"Assuming what you say is true,
  I will just take a short-cut through;
On my cornflakes, forever more,
  Straight Jack Daniels I will pour."

*Slightly embellished but
based on communiques between
friend Dominic Job and TV's
Charlie Chase.*

THE PHANTOM STEER

They seared his hide and cropped his ear,
   Then slapped his rump and said, "Little steer,
Go find your mommy, drink lots of milk,
   And keep your hair as soft as silk;
We'll see you in about four years
   When we gather in our shipping steers."

Now Little Steer's feelings were most forlorn,
   Worse than the trauma when he was born;
Back then his mommy filled his dream,
   Curried him off and fed him cream;
Protected him from parasites
   And cuddled him on frosty nights.

But these here mauchos called cowboy,
  With rawhide rope, in all their joy,
Circled it round his brisket hair
  And he went flying through the air;
Yes, they bled his ear, scorched his hide,
  And dealt death to his natural pride.

Poor Little Steer, he gimpied off,
  Laid down with a wheezened cough;
His mommy found him, coaxed him up,
  She licked his wounds and gave him sup;
But as he hurt he thought the more,
  Someday he would even the score.

Wounds healed up and Little Steer played,
  He romped in the sun and snoozed in the shade;
He drank lots of milk, ate green grass,
  And as the snows and springs did pass
He grew to be a handsome steer,
  But he ne'er let a cowboy near.

More than four years the pokes did ride,
  But never saw that steer's sleek hide;
By day he hid in brush and trees,
  At night he grazed in gentle breeze;
In all their rides the most they found
  Was his big footprint in the ground.

The years went by and time held sway,
  His face grew flecked, his hair turned gray;
His horns grew long as eagle's wings,
  His beller louder than a king's;
But never did those pokes get near,
  By then they called him Phantom Steer.

They then conjured to set a trap,
  So built a corral round the water gap;
Phantom knew he should seek a change
  But he hated to leave his old home range;
Needing a drink he dashed his pride
  And entered the trap in risk of his hide.

As he lowered to drink that moonlit night,
 Sixteen cowboys swung into sight;
They slammed the gate, circled the corral,
 Cocksure they now would end the spell;
Phantom took off and cleared the rail,
 One loop settled over his tail.

But another circled around his neck,
 The rider said 'whoa' to his big bay deck;
When Phantom hit the end of the line
 It snapped as though it was wrapping twine;
That old gray steer streaked for Dunn hill,
 As far as we know he is grazing still.

Some cowboys claim he's up on high
    Grazing the clouds there in the sky;
Flying around on silver wings,
    His beller as soft as an angel sings;
Some s'pect he's 'mong the Deity
    Grazing the lush 'neath an Eden tree.

Could Phantom be guarding those Pearly Gates,
    Himself deciding who matriculates?
If Phantom is working that cutting chute
    With his judgment determined absolute,
For those buckaroos Hell may be in store,
    Unless he opts to negate that score.

So when you leave this earthly abode,
  And approach the forks in that far away road,
If you happen to hear a snort and a blow
  And see a tail ringin' that's not quite slow,
You'll soon discover you'll be bunkin' in
  The heat and smoke and the fire's din.

Where soogans will be of little use,
  And you won't need jackets lined with goose;
Where Satan's prod has a multi-prong,
  And your labors be hard and hot and long;
Then you'll know you transgressed along the way
  And that Phantom Steer is having his say.

Just had a dream and it
wouldn't quit playin'.

AN OLD COWBOY'S DILEMMA

Casey rapped on his neighbor's door
  And entered when he heard "Come in";
Took his ease on a grubbox chair,
  Offered Charlie a cheery grin.

He and his friend chatted along,
  And shared a pot of Arbuckle brew;
They reminisced of days long past,
Two worn out pokes from the Rafter 2.

Their thoughts eventually turned to Jim,
  Tough as rawhide, honest and free;
Lived close to nature on the range,
  His background was the Lazy T.

They related a tale about him,
  Fourth of July that went amiss;
It happened in his waning years,
  No joke to him, it went like this:

Jim was standing on the boardwalk
  Waiting for the parade to start;
He had found a choice location
  And was reluctant to depart.

But nature called and Jim took off,
  A far lightpole was his utmost,
So he turned his back to windward
  And watered down that old lamp post.

The constable, with eagle eye,
  Spied that old cowboy in despair;
He threw Jim in the city clink,
  Booked for polluting ground and air.

Next morning Jim's before the court,
    "Seven days jail with fine to pay";
Then the judge inquires of old Jim
    If he might have anything to say?

"Just this, yer Honor," Jim laments,
    "You can enter it in yer log;
I've paid tax for forty years but still
    Ain't got the privilege of a dog."

A true story as told in the
Montana Journal. Happened
in Red Lodge, Montana.

JUST A WORKIN' BUCKAROO

I don't flash a silver buckle,
  Nor do I sit a hand-tooled kack;
My trottin' bag for shirts and jeans
  Is nothin' but a gunny sack.

My head don't fit a ten-X brim,
  And argyle socks are not for me;
I wear bandanas 'round my gullet,
  And croon my songs to steer and tree.

My pony's not of hot blood stock,
  He foaled out on and knows the range;
Of all the mounts I've seen around
  I would not one for him exchange.

Have my boots handmade by Justin,
  My chaps are Heiser cut and sewn;
Spurs, I have a cavvy of 'em,
  And each sounds a different tone.

Crawl from my soogans 'fore daylight,
  I take some chow and on my way;
Mount my buckskin for the roundup,
  Ridin' circle, long is the day.

Draw my pay and head for Shorty's,
  I buy a bath and barber shave;
Do all the bars and faro games,
  Then leave town broke with grin and wave.

Am bashful of those pretty girls,
  But I sure love 'em just the same;
If I e'er get myself a spread
  I'll play that girlie cooin' game.

But for now it's bean and biscuits,
  Hear that range cook roust the crew;
Grow another saddle callous,
  I'm just a workin' buckaroo. ↵

Yes, and they are real honest-to-goodness callouses, too.

IN NEED OF A JOB

I am just an old time waddie,
  Proddin' bulls has been my game;
Now I'm lookin' for some new range
  To ply my rustlin' fame.

I pack a mean rawhide riatta,
  It sings and settles true;
And the runnin' iron I carry
  Is always white-hot blue.

Don't you think that range where Boesky
  Went on his gaming spree
Would want for his replacement
  A waddie such as me?

My chaps and saddle are in soak,
  But I can drive them cars;
I can furnish my own bedroll
  And sleep beneath the stars.

For wages I ain't worried,
  I'll take a paltry sum;
Seven figures left of decimal
  And don't forget the rum.

Now the likker I ain't used to,
  Pinstripes I simply loathe;
But with that egging on the pay side
  I might attune to both. ↵

*Boesky served time for
his Wall Street antics.
That is one experience I
can do without.*

WALL STREET

THE BULL AND THE BEAR

Been a cowman all my livin',
   By chance I met Wall Street;
I thought that feller peddling stock
   Was selling red steer meat.

Thus the greatest ride I ever took
   Was on a Wall Street bear;
It went around but mostly down,
   Borne chiefly by hot air.

Now mean horses I've rode plenty,
   You ear 'em down to start;
Then climb aboard and sink your spurs,
   It is a work of art.

A brahma bull is tougher yet,
   Just first-rate hands can stay aboard;
Their skin is loose, they're quick as sin,
   They'll stomp you, leave you gored.

Wall Street bulls are a snap to ride,
   Just drop some greenbacks in the well;
But when they will turn to bear meat
   Is often hard to tell.

That Wall Street bull I straddled once,
   He went plumb out of sight;
Time he came down and hit hardpan
   He was a bear a'fight.

But that Wall Street bear was funny,
   There was no mane to grab;
Hustlers had him roached plumb slick,
   No handhold 'round to nab.

He didn't twist or sunfish much,
  He depended on sheer speed;
By time he hit the bottom rung
  I could feel my innards bleed.

"Ride the bull up and then get off,"
  Is sound advice, alright;
But what's to ride on the way down,
  How do you switch in flight?

Believe I prefer the brahma kind,
  Bulls wrapped in hide and hair;
They don't pretend to be your friend,
  Then dump you in despair. ↳

2700

2400

1100

*Sent this to the Wall Street
Journal but they refused to
publish it.*

STRIKING IT RICH

Did you ever dream of striking it rich,
  Of uncovering that mother lode;
Of finding a lead so deep and so wide
  Your eyeballs would simply explode?

Did you ever think of having a spread
  That reached clear from here to the coast;
One that could carry 'bout ten thousand head
  Of the best bloodlines you could boast?

Did you ever want for a championship,
  Steer wrestling or riding a bull;
Or roping a calf in world record time,
  Winning money by bucketsful?

Now if these are things you are dreaming of
  Better get on your working duds,
It sure takes lots of blood, sweat and luck
  To 'cumulate those kinds of spuds.

But there is another kind of richness
  That with some luck you just might find,
And if you do it's worth more than the wealth
  Of surely any other kind.

I stumbled upon a real nugget true,
  Of more carat than I deserved;
But she's coddled me and I'm hanging on
  'Till the Lord or she comes unnerved.

We hitched double-harness away back when,
  I had little to grant her life;
But she's made the most of that which I gave,
  And she's been a wonderful wife. ↵

After 48 years she's still
puttin' up with me.

—64—

WRANGLIN' WITH THEM SHE-DUDES

Dude wranglin's been with ranchin'
  Here in the West for years;
Since barb wire fenced the ranges
  And black ponies took on gears.

A train load of dudes and she-dudes,
  ('Twas the she-dudes I liked best);
They'd migrate from them eastern towns
  To give cowboyin' a test.

They would come plumb dressed in glitter,
  All togged out mane to toe;
High heeled boots and clankin' spurs,
  Big hat and all the show.

Their know-how of the ridin' game
  Wouldn't fill a durham sack;
They were as green as wagon paint
  When it came to a rawhide kack.

Their queries went about like this:
  Which side to mount the brutes?
What end to put the bridle on?
  Where is the horn that toots?

They asked about the steering wheel,
  And the brake on this old nerd?
They figured that a martingale
  Was just another kind of bird.

The nomenclature of a saddle
  Proved to be some devilish;
A stirrup to them she-dudes
  Had always been a kitchen dish.

And a curb was next to gutter,
  A skirt, to cover up their flesh;
When I mentioned 'bout a flank cinch
  They thought I was gettin' fresh.

They heard me talk of saddle bags,
  And became somewhat irate;
In referrin' to a padded seat
They thought me speakin' of their weight.

Then when I said a pair of swells
  Was only fer to grip,
They would have pumped me full of lead
  If there'd been a pistol on a hip.

Those she-dudes got sore and gimpy
  After ridin' trail a while;
Some stove up so bad they hoofed it,
  Leadin' pony single file.

Their new boots would then start rubbin',
  By time to camp they'd get
They couldn't tell which hurt the worst,
  Their feet or where they set.

But by end of dudin' season
  Those gals were ridin' mighty cute;
And some had the spunk and mustard
  To come spurrin' out the chute.

To say I didn't love 'em
  Would be a lizzard belly lie;
And I often dreamed that some day
  One might hitch this wrangler guy. ↵

*Lots of cuties among 'em,
but I got the cream of the
crop and she "warn't no she-
dude."*

THE SMARTEST DEAL I EVER MADE

I got into a shootin' scrape,
   Two pistols barked as one;
Hot lead split the atmosphere,
   My opponent dropped his gun.

My heart it skipped a beat or two
   When I heard a thuddy sound;
I reeled and spun, thought I was done,
   But I didn't hit the ground.

A partner grabbed me by the arm,
   He took me for a stroll;
I sipped a drink and didn't leak
   So figured I was whole.

My adversary did the same
   In a saloon across the street;
He couldn't find no crimson stuff
   A drippin' on his feet.

The thing that saved my bacon
   Was a rosette on my cuff;
His charm of life was nothin' more
   Than a tin can full of snuff.

I met him later man to man,
   We shook hands as real men do;
We discussed the facts before us,
   And the luck that saw us through.

Our difference was a female
   Dressed in fancy leotards;
We decides right there between us,
   Next time we'll cut the cards!!   ↵

It coulda happened at the
Dirty Shame, the Jersey Lilly
or the Lonesome Dove; and I
don't tell my wife everything.

BOWLEGGED PETE

Cowboy Pete was tall and skinny,
  Had a face like a tomahawk;
His nose and ears and chin as well
  Would make a jackass gawk.

His legs were long like sled runners,
  And bowed like barrel staves;
But when he mounted a salty horse
  He sure could ride the waves.

Once he was breakin' a little dun
  That shimmied just like jelly;
He'd swing off that bronc at every jump
  And kick him in the belly.

Good bronc riders always had
  Legs with the proper crook;
With tied down spurs hooked in a cinch,
  That's most of what it took.

But for catchin' pigs those bowlegs
  Was a handicap in disguise;
One time Pete was helping us
  Catch a shoat of considerable size.

We cornered him and were moving in
  When he turned toward Pete with a stare;
He spied the light and shot the gap,
  And never mussed a hair.

We heard Pete's heels a clickin',
  But his knees just couldn't close;
To this day, so far as I know,
  That hog's still rootin' with his nose.

*Wright Harvey was one of the
best bronc riders that ever
hit the Musselshell.*

COWBOYS, COCKLEBURS AND CROW BAIT

A band of sheep a-blattin'
Ain't the music of cows lowin',
But often it's a band of sheep
That has kept that cowman goin'.

Most cowboys won't admit
To ever having milked a cow;
When the need to do arises
They simply say they don't know how.

A cowboy lamented to his friend,
"I've a thorn on my hands, a real cocklebur";
Said the friend to the cowboy,
"Maybe you shouldn't have married her."

The anatomy of a horse from withers to toes
Tells if he's good for work or only repose;
A rule of thumb that's been used since Mo'es,
It's a legend 'mong cowboys, like this it goes:
"Four white feet with stripe down his nose,
Cut off his head and throw it to the crows."

Stories of old but
poetry original.

THE DAY MY SADDLE HORN BLEW OFF

Now wind is part of the weather,
  It's discussed every day of the week;
But you'd best not listen to what's bein' said
  If it's only the truth that you seek.

The Dakotas have problems at times,
  A dust storm is not that serene;
They run guide wires from porch to privy
  To avoid getting lost in between.

Crop rotation's no problem in Idaho,
  Along the Snake's great watershed;
Spud farmers don't rotate their crops,
  The wind moves the soil instead.

Those Okies who live around Tulsa
  Have to pay taxes in Kansas state;
That is where their topsoil blows to
  At a fast and furious rate.

In Nebraska, believe it or not,
  At a town on the North Platte road,
A hurricane dropped outa the sky
  And messed up the local zip code.

And Kansans who farm around Newton
  See their topsoil blow like scat;
A stranger was known to have choked to death
  By the chin strap on his hat.

Now the wind never blows in Barstow,
  The sand just relocates on its own;
If Winchester could harness those rockets
  It would replace lead bullets with stone.

There are spots in Nevada, I'm told,
  Where the breeze blows in flurries right strange;
It can clean out your purse in seconds,
  Without leaving you coffee change.

They say there's 'hot' air in Texas,
  And it sure as Hades can blow;
That's what thaws the Yukon country
  After a winter of sixty below.

If the wind doesn't blow 'round Cheyenne,
  Why does it blow in surrounding states?
It may be those Wyoming cowboys
  Have the good sense to close their gates.

Arizona has sights that are gorgeous,
  Mixed among the mesquite and spruce;
But the snowbirds soon learn first hand
  That those deserts can move like a goose.

There's an area in southern Montana
  Where wind gauges can't measure the storm;
At times it blows harder than others,
  And the adverse is deemed the norm.

After one trickle of air down the canyon
  All the culverts were standing on end;
And the railroad tunnel through the hill
  Took on a considerable bend.

A rancher was out settin' fence posts
  When a stiff breeze came driftin' through;
It inverted all of his post holes
  And bent his spud bar clean in two.

But the worst blow I ever was in
  Dropped my horse in a quag of quicksand;
I landed upstream about four miles
  With that saddle horn still in my hand.

*Blame this wind onto being
born under the zodiac sign of
Taurus the Bull, then raised
in the Bull mountains.*

HOW I GOT MY NAME

Some babes' names get handed down
　　From generations of the past;
Some are named for presidents
　　Whose fame will ever last.

Some are born 'mong sterile walls
　　Between sheets of warm frieze;
I didn't see such luxuries,
　　But I darn sure came to stay.

I was born on a wet saddle blanket
　　In the shade of a scrub pine tree;
Where bobcats and buzz snakes abound,
　　Near the head of Carter's coulee.

My mom was out checking cattle
　　When she felt the first tinge of pain;
She headed for camp but I kicked,
　　So she had to pull in the rein.

She slipped the saddle and blanket,
　　And told Boomer to go eat grass,
But not to stray too far afield
　　Because 'fore long her pain would pass.

Soon she slapped my rump and I howled,
　　Breathed my first of Cherry Springs air;
She knew right then that all was well,
　　That she had a cowhand for fair.

She's about to call me Chester
　　When she spied this here Jimson weed;
She named me Jim for that poison plant,
　　Then whistled for her grazing steed. ↵

*Can't vouch for the truth of
this. I was there but don't
remember. See Webster for
definition of Jimson weed.*

FRIEND ALLEN

He was tall and dark and handsome
  With a clear twinkle in his eye,
And the curl in his friendly smile
  Was sincere but verged on the sly.

When he shook my hand the first time
  I knew it was man-to-man,
For he had that air about him
  That only a true fellow can.

He loved his family and friends,
  Spoke well of all he knew;
He traveled tall in the saddle,
  And cared for nature, too.

He promised me a loony*,
  And gave it to me last spring;
Just a token of friendship,
  A luck-in-your-pocket thing.

I shall keep and cherish it long,
  Mixed with my nickels and dimes;
Right where I finger it daily,
  And think of friend Allen each time.

We knew this poet but shortly,
  Still felt close as a friendship can;
We're bound to be better people
  For knowing this gifted man.

There's a sadness about us right now,
  God mixes the good with the sad;
But as one's own life progresses
  We remember the good that we've had.

*Canadian dollar

Yes, there's a void in my heart today
  That can never be filled again,
But consider myself as privileged
  To have been able to call him my friend.

A new Canadian acquaintance.
It sure hurts to lose a good
one like him.

THIS BARD'S WIFE

She listens to the first draft
  And she listens to the last,
There's a dozen in-betweeners
  That her judgment on she's passed.

She dassent do no talkin'
  Until first she's spoken to,
Lest she interrupts an idee
  That he's a-pluckin' from the blue.

She helps him with his adjectives,
  Gives action to his verbs,
She offers up some titles,
  And soothes all his disturbs.

When the danged thing's finally finished,
  If there are accolades to strew,
There is only one name on 'em
  You know who they're written to.

Still she follows him all over
  Helpin' gather in his cheers,
But if the truth were noted
  They're not just his, but theirs.

Cause a picture ain't worth nothin'
  Until the trim is set in place;
It's the finish that it's judged on,
  That's what earns it the embrace. ⌐

*There is no fiction in this
one.*

AN INCIDENT IN THE ROUND CORRAL

It was on a frosty morning
  In the springtime long ago,
That two partners, Walt and Joe,
  Were due to stage a cowboy show.

They had a bunch of four-year-olds
  That needed breakin' on their spread,
So they headed for the round corral
  To see what might lay ahead.

The wrangler had one all cut out,
  Walt thought aloud, "I'm breakin' you";
But before the ride was over
  Walt was broken smack in two.

He had four stocking leggins,
  And sure was full of fight;
A polecat stripe ran down his nose,
  The rest was black as anthracite.

Now partner Joe, he eared him down
  While Walt cinched on the leather;
Walt climbed aboard and nodded,
  He surmised some stormy weather.

That blackie hoss, he blew a snort,
  Gave Walt scant time to spare;
He dropped a curtsy with his nose,
  Then he began to groom the air.

He bellered like a billy goat
  As he combed the atmosphere;
And when his footsies graced the ground
  He grunted like a bear.

As he pawed those upper reaches
  And plowed that ground below,
Walt said later that he wondered
  If he should not let go.

But he didn't need to wonder
  'Cause it happened just the same;
He lost all contact with that horse,
  It was now a brand new game.

Walt hit that terra firma
  Where hoss hadn't plowed at all;
The lights went out real pronto
  As those stars began to fall.

When he came to 'twas morning,
  He was in a trundle bed;
A nurse was pattin' at his hand
  And holdin' cold packs on his head.

He thought he was in Heaven,
  So he checked for wings on her;
Then he felt a splitting headache,
  Saw visions of old Lucifer.

He spent some thirty days
  With that little nurse so cute;
Before that time was up
  His love for her was absolute.

But she proved to be elusive
  As most young heifers are,
So all he had for memory
  Was a heart with one more scar.

As for that hoss named Anthracite,
  He got throwed in the outlaw pen;
While Walt went back on bunkhouse chow,
  And astraddle his saddle again.

My dad, Joe Ross, and his friend, Walter Wallace, were early day partners in the horse business.

A LESSON LEARNED—CHECK BOTH ENDS

I didn't steal that fella's horse,
  I didn't steal a horse, I say!
I just screwed out a picket pin
  And slowly strode away;
I didn't know that picket rope
  Packed a critter that eats hay.

He didn't whinny, nicker,
  I never heard him neigh;
There was no tuggin' on that rope
  As I blithely went my way;
So how was I to know
  I had a critter that eats hay?

When once I reached the willers
  As the dawning light turned gray,
I peeked a casual gander
  From whence I came my way;
There trailed that lovely critter
  That lives on oats and hay.

By now I'm nearing home,
  And I've hungered on the way,
I'll return him to his owner
  Some later in the day;
So I put him in a box stall
  And gave him oats and hay.

They would not accept my story
  So now I'm in a hoosegow bay,
And the vittles ain't too pleasin',
  Those that grace my dinner tray;
They're not near as appetizing
  As that critter's oats and hay.

So I offer these conclusions
  That I've gleaned along the way:
"Don't make no snappy judgments,
  And don't no hanky-panky play;
Don't fool with others' critters
  That live on oats and hay."

Wrote this as a sequel to a
previous poem titled
"Cojutatin' Time".

—85—

THERE ARE JEANS AND THERE ARE GENES

Jeeter had on some new black jeans,
　　Just came from the toggery store;
Size he called, "Forty-two let out;
　　They fit better than forty-four."

Was that why he bought forty-twos,
　　'Stead of the costlier forty-four?
His staunch ancestral history
　　Had oftentimes surfaced before.

With alterations free of charge,
　　And with a price break in between,
He wasn't fooling that store gent,
　　Jeeter's Scotch genes glowed with a sheen.

*Jeeter didn't make the rules
so he couldn't be blamed for
taking advantage of them.*

A RANCH CHRISTMAS OF LONG AGO

When Thanksgiving's feast was over
    And the snow started settlin' in
We youngsters grabbed the catalogs,
    Choosing gifts for the toy bin.

What each would like from Santa,
    Always a tough and strenuous task;
To pick and choose, eliminate,
    For the things from him we'd ask.

Then we each would write a letter
    Informing him how good we'd been,
And listing all of our desires,
    From bicycle to bantam hen.

Chances are the older ones
    Knew how Santa got his gifts,
But we werent' told till Christmas eve
    That he would have a change of shifts.

He would delay our house call,
    There were poor kids far away,
He first would visit them,
    Give them gifts on Christmas day.

That Christmas eve we gathered round
    While Mom retold the Savior theme,
Played the organ and sang carols,
    And we made some rich snow cream.

Dad had wheat in the granary,
    Two teams of horses in the stall,
But fourteen miles in two-foot snow
    Was just too tough a haul.

He saw money in the future,
    But now he didn't have a dime,
So our orders to old Santa
    Just had to sit and bide their time.

'Twas a few days after Christmas
    When the snow settled down real neat,
Just right for winter sledding,
    So Dad loaded up his wheat.

Next morning he left early,
    That night Santa came our way;
Dad said he saw those reindeer
    Heading north with empty sleigh.

Well, I don't recall the outcome,
    What presents each kid got,
But we all were smiles and happy
    With what old Santa brought.

When that Christmas comes to mind
    I reminisce a set,
Cause there's no doubt it had to be
    The sweetest Christmas yet.

True, as I recall it after
sixty-some years.

HIGHER EDUCATION

The Prof was oratin', givin' us a heap
  On how to make money on a cow and a sheep,
When up jumped a lad from out in the sticks
  Who wished to get in a few personal licks.

He said he had come to a total impasse,
  Tryin' to hitch up an ox with an ass;
He'd seen it done once in the Tarheel state,
  They was progressin' at a steady gait.

Ass in the furrow, beside him the cow,
  With the farmer workin' the walkin' plow;
He hadn't noticed right there on the spot,
  Was they hitched by yoke, two collars, or what.

Also botherin' both he and his maw,
  How to saw straight with a lousy Swede saw;
In buildin' a corral or workin' up wood,
  That damned Swede saw just wasn't no good.

Modern machines have cured both this boy's ills,
  Likely by now he's got off them nerve pills;
The tractor replaced the ox and the ass,
  The Swede saw's done in by one run on gas.

When it's nice and warm you can get by fine,
  Can plow straight furrows and saw a straight line;
But times of the year these new tools raise hob
  In makin' some money and completin' a job.

My throttle finger workin' that chain saw
  Chills something like sin when in winter's raw;
Except for my hands I can keep warm,
  But gloves are as cold as an icicle storm.

When the wind is a howlin' at forty below,
  And I'm up to my belt in blue powder snow,
I wish that professor would explain it to me,
  How to keep my hands warm while fallin' a tree. ↵

There are problems encountered in everyday life that school learning doesn't ever address.

LIKE MY PONY, IT GETS ME THERE

Some folks tour in automobiles,
  While I just drive a Ford;
I'll dote on it until I go
  To reap my just reward.
Some folks dine on caviar,
  But I'll take beef cooked rare;
There's nothing beats a juicy steak
  On my old bill-o-fare.

Some folks tour in automobiles,
  While I just drive a Ford;
I love to hear that motor hum,
  And I like a running board.
Some folks need twelve cylinders,
  They think that's sheer pizzazz;
But I get along with four putt-putts,
  That's what my milk cow has.

Some folks tour in automobiles,
  While I just drive a Ford;
That rumble seat is the very thing
  My mother-in-law adored.
Some folks wear fancy ostrich boots,
  I wear those working things;
If I was meant to be a bird
  I would have sprouted wings.

Some folks tour in automobiles,
    While I just drive a Ford;
Others buy fancy foreign makes,
    I'll stick with Henry's horde.
Some folks lunch on three martinis,
    But I eat spuds and squash;
My belly likes those solids, it
    Don't need no likker wash.

Some folks tour in automobiles,
    While I just drive a Ford;
I fancy those old T's and A's,
    Even though they're not restored.
Some folks' 'johns' are tiled and shagged,
    But mine don't even flush;
A Wards catalog is all it needs,
    It don't take no bowl brush.

Some folks tour in automobiles,
    While I just drive a Ford;
When driving my old Twenty-nine
    I hear a heavenly chord.
Some folks copycat the Joneses,
    But I'm just Cowboy Jim;
I live on beans and sow belly,
    My longjohns ain't got lace trim.

Some folks tour in automobiles,
    While I just drive a Ford;
And guess I'll keep on doin' that
    'Till I go meet the Lord. ⌐

My first car was a '29 Model A
coupe. Bought it in 1942 for
$82.00.

THE SQUARE AND COMPASS

I was just a maverick drifting,
  My head half in the sand,
When I fell in with a well marked bunch
  Who wore a common brand.

They asked in whom I placed my trust?
  I said it was with God;
So they cast their ballots with me,
  Marked me with their branding rod.

They dressed me in white lambskin,
  Informed me of their working tools;
They admonished me to live
  By their teachings and their rules.

With precepts good and wholesome,
  They honor womanhood;
And through their youngster programs
  They do a heap of good.

Their bunkhouse is not spacious,
  But in member's hearts it's grand;
The rich and poor sit side-by-side,
  Trail boss is just another hand.

If you want to wear their markings,
  To live and with them graze,
Best check in at their cutting chute,
  They don't go rounding up the strays.

Yes, I wear the square and compass,
  And though my brand's grown dim of late,
Those markings won't be vented
  Until I reach God's home ranch gate. ⌐┘

*A great fraternal group that
has counted many U.S. presidents
as members, including
George Washington.*

BEANS

That staple in the grub wagon
  Sure packed a mighty punch,
And every cookshack in the West
  Stocked 'em by the bunch;
If cowboys knew not "what's for chow"
  Beans was a surefire hunch.

Hardtack and beans and sow belly,
  That's all there was to eat;
And when there wasn't sow belly
  Beans took the place of meat;
They ate beans boiled and fried and souped
  And munched 'em in their sleep.

'Twas beans for breakfast and for 'sup'
  With bean pie in betweens;
If Taco John thinks he was first
  to try those refried beans
He should have eaten roundup grub
  To help hold up his jeans.

Now there's pintos and great northerns
  And there are limas, too;
There are navys and mo' wonders
  And some are black-eyed sue;
But give me red ones, they're my forte,
  I like that crimson hue.

Just cover them in water
  With a hamhock bone or two,
Or a piece of old salt pork or
  A bacon rind will do;
Then set 'em on the hind stove lid
  And give 'em time to stew.

You can serve 'em up a steamin'
  (They're 'bout as good plumb cold),
But regardless how you take 'em
  They'll fill out your belly fold;
They will stick to your old ribbing
  Like bedrock sticks to gold.

Beans sustained cowpokes and soldiers
  As o'er the plains they led,
So give me beans, the Royal food,
  And I prefer mine RED;
If there's a bit of pork in them
  I'll deem myself well fed.

So when I serve my time on earth,
  Can no longer fork my bay;
When I can no more roll my bed,
  God wills I've had my stay,
Just give me a pot of Red beans
  And I'll be on my way. ⌐

*If there is better chow than
red beans and sowbelly with
hot biscuits I have yet to
taste it.*

THE END

As you've traveled o'er these passages
  It's the author's fervent hope
That your journey was most pleasant
  At an easy, gentle lope.

Now that you've ridden full circle,
  Have come to the finis, the end,
May your saddle sores be few enough
  To continue to call me your friend.

                    J.A.R.

*Until we meet again,
so long.*

THE ILLUSTRATOR

Mary Jane Ross, daughter of the author, has many talents, and one of them is definitely art. Most of her hobbies pertain to art in one form or another. In addition to illustrating books, she does wood carving, china painting and stained glass work.

Before she ever started to school she was putting together little books about birds and flowers. After illustrating these books, she would dictate to her mother an accompanying story. Her mother would print the stories as dictated to her. Then Mary Jane would copy the printing into her books. They are prized possessions today.

Mary Jane lives with her husband, Bill Bradt, and their two young sons at Hamilton, Montana where she is employed at the Rocky Mountain Federal Health Laboratory.

THE AUTHOR

Jim Ross was born under the zodiac sign of Taurus the Bull. Complementing that he spent his first eighteen years on a ranch in the Bull Mountains of Musselshell County, Montana. Through the years, to provide for his wife and five children, he did a number of things, including ranching. In semi-retirement, he and his wife now reside on a small irrigated ranch in the Bitterroot Valley of Montana. In addition to operating the place, he spends considerable time writing and publishing his poetry.